How Bill Found Rain

by Susan McCloskey
illustrated by Tim Ellis

Scott Foresman

Editorial Offices: Glenview, Illinois • New York, New York
Sales Offices: Reading, Massachusetts • Duluth, Georgia
Glenview, Illinois • Carrollton, Texas • Menlo Park, California

Mom said, "It has been too hot!"
Dad said, "It has been too dry!"

Sis said, "It has been too sunny.
We need rain.
What can we do?"

Bill said, "We do need rain!
And I will get it."

"I will show you," said Bill.
"But first I need rope.
Lots of rope!"

Mom found some rope.
Dad found some rope.
Sis found some rope.

Bill found some rope too.
Then Bill rode off.

Bill rode and rode.

First he rode here.

Then he rode there.

He was looking for something.

And he found it!
It was big and black.
It was a cloud!

Bill got his new rope.
He threw it at the cloud.

He got it!
He got it on the first try.

Bill pulled and tugged.
He tugged and pulled.
That cloud was big!

He pulled the cloud home.

"Bill is home!" Sis said.

"Oh," Bill said.
"I have been here.
 I have been there.
 And look what I found!"

Bill pulled hard on the rope.

Mom felt a drip.

Dad felt a drop.

Sis felt a drip and a drop.

She gave Bill a kiss.

And that is how Bill found rain.